Polar Bear Babies

Gina Cline and Traci Dibble

 There is snow here.

There is ice here. It is cold.

3

 The polar bear lives here.

She has lots of fur.
She will not be cold.

6

Her fur looks white. It looks white like the snow.

To have her baby, she will make a house of snow.

She will sleep. 9

 She will have her baby in a snow house.

The baby is so little.

 Many polar bears have two babies.
Some have one, three, or four babies.

This mother had one baby. 13

She and her baby will be in the snow house for many, many days.

The mother will not eat.
She will give the baby milk. 15

They come out of the snow house.

Now, the baby is not so little.

The mom has to eat.
The baby has to go with her.

She will look for seals to eat.

To get big, the baby has
to have lots of seals to eat.
Her mother gets seals for her.

Then, she shows her baby
how to get seals.

 When the baby is three, the baby will have to get seals for herself.

Where are the seals?
Will they get to eat?

23

The Polar Bear's Snow House

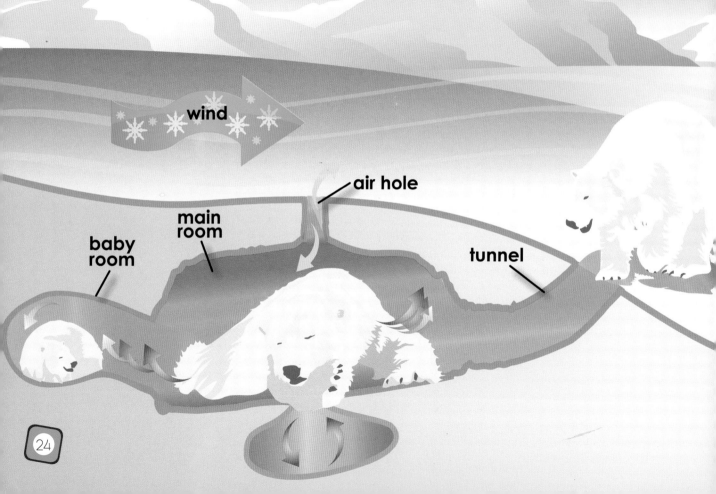

wind

air hole

baby room

main room

tunnel

The Polar Bear's Life Cycle

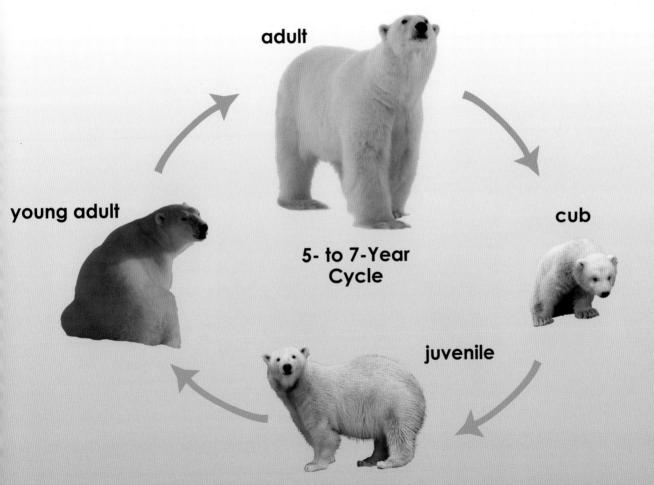

adult

young adult

5- to 7-Year
Cycle

cub

juvenile

The Polar Bear Lives Here

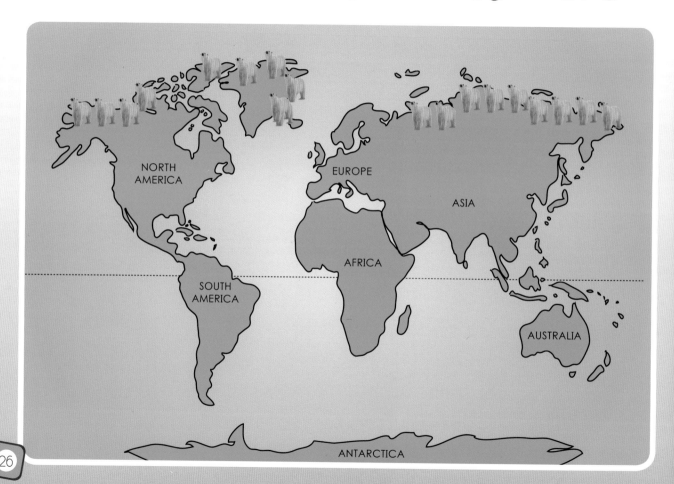

The Polar Bear Food Web

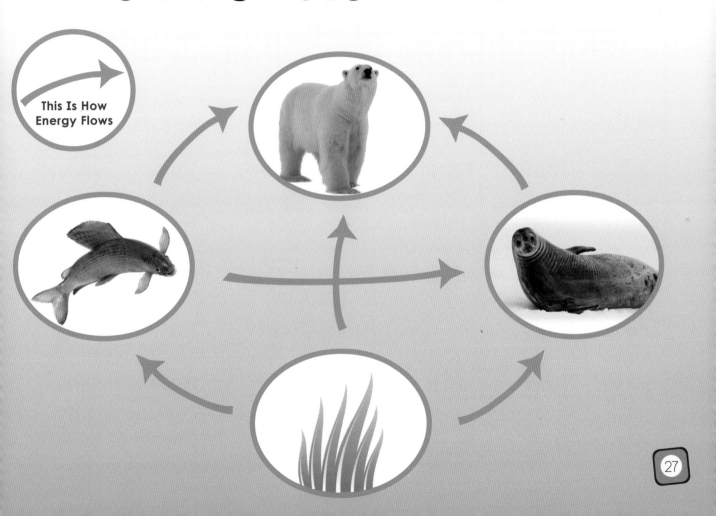

This Is How Energy Flows

Power Words

How many can you read?

a	eat	have	like	mother	so	to
and	for	her	little	not	some	two
are	four	here	live	now	the	when
baby	get	house	look	of	then	where
be	give	how	lots	one	there	white
big	go	in	make	or	they	will
come	had	is	many	out	this	with
day	has	it	mom	she	three	